Manufacturing America

Poems from the Factory Floor

Lisa Beatman

Ibbetson Press · Somerville, Massachusetts · 2008

Ibbetson Press · Somerville, Massachusetts · 2008

Cover photo and others by Lisa Beatman.
Inside back cover photo by Richard Yoder.

ISBN 978-0-6151-8124-0
First printing — January 2008
Printed in USA.

for Rick

who taught me the poetry
of cogs and circuits

Acknowledgements

Grateful acknowledgement to the editors of the
following publications where these poems first
appeared:

Hazmat Review: "Good Bones"

Howling Dog Press: "76 Properzi Way, Somerville"
"Citizen Delia," "Crumbs", "Manufacturing
America," "Nursery"

Ibbetson Review: "Hack"

Pemmican Press: "New Mexico," "Rainbow," "First
Shift," Swing Shift," Hand Operator," "What We
Bring With Us."

Political Affairs: "Scrap"

Heartfelt appreciation to Sacatar Foundation in Brazil,
the Writers' Colony at Dairy Hollow in Arkansas,
the Dorland Mountain Arts Colony in California,
the Dorset House in Vermont, Kalani Honua in
Hawaii, and the Tyrone Guthrie Center and Salmon
Publishing in Ireland.

Many thanks to poetry mentors Pam Bernard, Ted
Baxter, Harris Gardner, Doug Holder, and Marc
Widershien. A toast to Saturday mornings with the
Jamaica Pond Poets writers' group.

Contents

Foreward 9
New World 12
New Mexico 17
Sticks of Bamboo 18
Rainbow 20
First Shift 21
Hand Operator 22
Santa Benigna del Carmen de la Cubeta 23
Needlework 24
Swing Shift 25
What We Bring With Us 26
Third Shift 27
Manufacturing America 28
Citizen Delia 30
Crumbs 32
Claudine's Deal 33
Krispy Kreme 34
Serpent 36
Coffee Break 38
Scrap 40
Hack Job 41
Parking 42
Good Bones 44
76 Properzi Way, Somerville 45
Nursery 46
Firing Uncle Hillel 48
Copyright 60

Foreward

In October 2001, I was hired by a paper and printing company to teach basic skills to the immigrants working on the factory floor. Employees from 41 countries worked there – in management, in sales, and in the heart of the manufacturing plant.

My students struggled to make their way. They worked hard. Most of them worked overtime; many of them had second jobs. A large number of them had fled from life-threatening political turmoil, with only the clothes on their backs. They were trying to make a life here, for themselves and their families. They paid taxes, attended local churches, and they celebrated both American holidays and the special feast days of their native lands: El Salvador, Haiti, Brazil, Uganda, Cambodia, Russia, Albania, Somalia, and the Azores, among them.

Manufacturing has been a traditional leg up for millions of American immigrants, including my own family, who came from Ukraine, Austria, and Germany. A doorway through which families could put food on their tables and books in their children's hands. Sadly, manufacturing is dying in America. Owners, seeking lower labor costs and fewer regulations, are relocating plants, ironically, to many of the developing countries their workers came from.

Here are their portraits.

Prologue

New World

The raggedy mouse jumped ship
and scuttled across cobblestones
into a dark doorway.
He shivered awhile
in a corner till
he got his land-paws.
This new world
was all coal-stink and pandemonium,
the shouts of men caught
by low ceilings and careened back,
twofold in strength.

He'd got used to the open air,
the see-sawing of waves,
since the schooner had
always found its center,
used to the daunting blue
above and green below,
the lovely reek of guano
and piles of fermenting fish-heads.

Here, it was dark overmuch
though gaslights bared the bones
of looms pumping night and day,
but there was food aplenty
dropped by the shadow figures
at their brief suppers,
crusts scented with the tall grass
of fields he'd almost put out of mind,
red rinds, sticky with Gouda,
and the new taste –
rich broth of knackered horses
boiled down into an irresistible paste.

The paper was gnawable,
though not the cream-vellum
from the old place,
and the bits of wool
carded and cast aside
were golden with lanolin,
seed husks yet lodged within,
but best of all
there was no ship's cat.

First Shift

New Mexico

The land was bread
a hard rusk that bore
the Mendez family's
teething pangs,
the Rio Grande curled,
fetal in its bends
clouded with silt,
an impoverished milk
that nonetheless
sustained them –
Ana, Miguel,
and la Chiquita
who rode on their backs
through the crossing-over
till she could take in
the whole-meal
of this new homeland
dry and hot
as an oven tempering
dirt and thorns
into loaves rising.

Sticks of Bamboo

On the back border I built my house
stilted on marshgrass and sedge
cock-crow I paddled to trawl the fish
dusk slid by patching my nets.

Now only the river will buy my house
only the Mekong enraged
banks of the fisherman cracked and sluiced
this my Vietnamese fate.

Built with the bamboo Grandfather grew
built by my father and me
floored with the bamboo laid flat in slats
bound loose for the fresh nighttime breeze.

Only the river will buy my house
only the Mekong uncaged
groves of Grandfather deluged in weeds.
bellied-up fish crowning waves.

If rivers can change their direction with time
then so must the dwellers abide.
a raft swollen with children floats
steered by prevailing tides.

Only the river will buy my house
only the Mekong assuaged
sticks of my house spin in eddies far
bones of my mothers submerged.

I cling to the raft of bamboo sticks
built by my brothers and me
built from the sticks of our roof and walls
masted by shirts and bedsheets.

Only the river will buy my house
only the Mekong grown strong
where will my people find shores to land
where will we build a new home?

Rainbow

In Santiago, Juan cast his net
on a rainbow lake, testing the patched weave,
gesturing with silent jerks of his jaw
for brother Rigoberto to hold fast
to the other end. Mottled catfish,
purplemouth grunts, and the red-breast tilapia
swam hard into Juan and Rigoberto's yawning net.

When the net broke for good, the brothers walked
to L.A., casting their arms through prickers
for ruby fruits, May strawberries,
July raspberries, moving from camp to camp
till they saved enough to join Aunt Ana
in Boston. Young Rigoberto was quick
with his new tongue, landing them jobs
making folders for the children's hospital.

Juan is mute as a lake, but he knows
his colors: purple is A-F,
blue is G-K, yellow is L-P,
red is Q-T, green is U-Z.
His calloused hands, tattooed with paper cuts
sort the folders that will hold each child's story.

First Shift

Nina puts her face
back on at 5:00 am
She cakes mascara on thick
to make her eyes big
they are small with sleep.

She reapplies
watermelon
tint to her lips
the upper slice
the lower one
and gives each
cheek a pinch
then stumbles out
of her dancing heels
and into an old
pair of Keds

Cut down
her feet take her
onto the factory floor
She goes to her post
and holds out her hands
Fresh-glued folders fly off
the conveyor belt
Catch, inspect, stack and pack
Catch, inspect, stack and pack
Her face dips and sways
She hums under her breath
The machine flirts back
Cha cha   cha cha cha

Hand Operator

Chitra applies her bookkeeping skills
to her new job, creasing each folder

with mathematical precision.
Six years since she took the red veil

and flew from Gujerat. She counts the days,
till her husband finds a sponsor

and sleeps in her bed. She counts the minutes,
till she can smoke in the break room

wrapped in the chatter of vending machines.
In her pockets, she counts her spare change.

Santa Benigna del Carmen de la Cubeta

Saint Beni of the bucket
starts at six
her hair a twisted black rag
her arms round as roasts
her feet chucks of wood.

She swabs the chief's toilet
till it gleams like a tooth
then shoulders the mop
to eleven more thrones.

No loaves or fishes
spring from her wand
but all that she scrubs
is made new.

Needlework

We gather in the break room
to embroider our fortunes
daily at 10:00.
Through confections
of cloth and yarn
we stitch our simple days
into leaves and petals,
tie off the frayed ends
and bite them with our teeth.

We gossip, it is true,
but only about
other Brazilians:
Eulampia, whose daughter
is in her tenth month.

Try erve-doce tea, says Rita,
Miralva says pray,
Graça the godmother just hums.
When it's time, it's time.
The little one is waiting –
call him, send an invitation,
rub Vera's belly with dendé oil,
hem him a diaper looped in gold
with his name.

Swing Shift

Alicia leaves the house at 2:00
Guillermo gets home at 4:00
Gracias a Dios
his mama can watch
Manuelito in between.
They feel lucky to work these shifts –
Doña Carmen is 68
and too tired to babysit all day
or all night, but she would
do anything for her grandbaby
Gracias a Dios
she doesn't have to.

Saturdays are trickier
They both work 7:00 – 3:00
and need the overtime
so Manuelito goes to church
with Doña Carmen.
She would like to spend more time
with the ladies and the Lord
but the baby is no Adventist –
he is wet and fussy
so she takes the rear pew
late and leaves early.

Alicia is Católica
She isn't pleased with Manuelito's
7th-Day Saturdays
but she loves Doña Carmen
for helping out
Manuelito spits up his formula
Doña Carmen wipes it off
his ruddy face and her turquoise dress.
She dabs her handkerchief
in the holy water
when no one's looking
Gracias a Dios.

What We Bring With Us

Beneath the loamy killing fields
Prak's father's bones articulate rice.

Beneath a fading Red Sox cap
Prak composts Cambodia.

His hands feed machines
to put wheat on the table.

His children will know grandfather
grain by grain.

Third Shift

Hands are tongues
on the graveyard shift
or are they wings?
Jacques' fingers flutter like doves
hovering by the die-cut machine
he motions to Abdul
to throw him a wrench.
A hammer?
Abdul's big fist
pounds a phantom nail.
Nyet – Nadya's index fingers
knife the butter air
as if assembling pie crusts.

Atman, Martir, Fatima, Areik,
the souls who work
the graveyard shift
bind books they cannot read
with fluent hands.

Manufacturing America

Yakov is a crackerjack
talks so fast he slurs his words.
Never one to wait in line
he shook his booty
when the Soviets crashed.
He's bent on being foreman
but the guys can't make him out.

Aleksei hustles the mailroom.
His filing system is a Mingus riff
but the boss don't like jazz.
He wanted to study philosophy
in New York City
but papa said
Moscow or New York
you still have to eat.

Misha drives the forklift
like an armored tank.
A good soldier
he was up to make colonel
but they "forgot"
to give him the exam.
It's ok, he says,
it is what it is.

Boris is 62.
He can fix old machines
but not his broken tongue,
so he draws pictures
of parts and procedures.
He wishes the English
were as easy as the radar system
on Mir. He had a hand in that.
At least, he has a job
and a small small apartment.
His wife watches Russian TV
and is always sad.

These Russian Jews
conjugate each Wednesday
in class at the paper factory.
They bite their lips to say 'visa' and 'vinegar'
They purse them to say 'want ads' and 'why.'

Citizen Delia

Delia is getting citizened up.
A samba-hipped woman
who wants to be a hyphenated-American.
She glues perma-clips on folders.
One by one. And grabs lunch on her feet.
Except for Tuesdays.
Pizza and Citizenship day.
Delia doesn't like pizza
but what can you do?

She opens 'Voices of Freedom.'
The old book has old presidents.
She learns the new ones on TV.
Everyone is excited for Delia.
She will be the first one.
The teacher wants to help
and has good ideas.
Be calm. Take your time.
Wear a suit.

Delia has another idea.
She already put her clothes out on the bed.
A red blouse down to here.
A black mini-skirt, short-short.
The new push-up bra.
In the store, Manuela the baby
said Mami your boobs are growing.
Good.
She hopes the immigration officer is a man.

Delia's eyes are raccoon-lined.
She likes her teacher.
Mrs. Gold would go in a suit.
Mrs. Gold says be confident, be comfortable.
Delia will be Delia
and she will pass the test.

Crumbs

Beneath the floorboards of industry
under the rattle and ho
mouse punches in.
He knows the building plan by heart --
no toe of the sprawling footprint
has gone unnibbled.

Not the old part
groaning with rot,
drafty and dim,
not the later additions
glaring with florescence,
studded with outlets
that can shock a mouse silly.
He rubs his nose

and runs up to the window rooms,
where the bosses breakfast
on flow-charts and croissants,
scuttles down to the cafeteria cupboards,
where Vietnamese temps
stash their tubs of salted rice,
scrabbles amongst the cubbies
of screechy secretaries,
desks strewn with melba toasts,
stained with diet coke,
and, daringly, darts around
the shop floor, where graveyard foremen
are tearing into tuna subs
on ten-minute breaks.
The 7:00 a.m. siren squeals
long after his shift.
Mouse always tries to punch
out before daylight,
leaving trails of nubbly pellets
to find his way home.

Claudine's Deal

Deep in a drawer
stuffed in a sock
lies a small gold circlet, edges worn,
modest stone mirroring the dark.

Page 5 of the Safety
Handbook states
no rings, no dangling chains,
no flowing hair. C'est rien.

So many moving parts,
tired rubber belts, rusted plates,
a woman bending over
her work has much to lose.

Better to miss the faint
warmth of a man,
the cling of children,
than a reddened finger, a worn arm.

Minding the rules
leaves half a paycheck
stuffed in a sock,
week by week,

growing wings
to fly home on a foreign
stamp, sparkling
in the Haitian sun.

Krispy Kreme

Un momento, Julio said,
sliding the starched apron strings
over his slick-backed hair. I come.
Don't say it – do it, and speak English!
Frank Martin said, his face a boiling vat
of oil. Frank wiped his glazed face.
Opening day, and he sure as hell
hadn't moved all the way north
to this cold snooty town to have
some dumb chico mess things up for him.
Ok, I here, what I do?
Julio had snuck up on him –
gonna have to look out for that one.

The glass front doors opened, and a great glob
of people fell through, separating out and lining up
like the donuts extruding onto the conveyor belt.
They were puffed and pale, the customers,
the donuts, and they were meant for each other,
just as Frank was meant to rise like yeast
through the ranks of Krispy Kreme
and Julio was meant to sweep and polish and lunch
on fried dough rejects and send half his pay,
little as it was, home to Rosario and Mama.

The day was rising.

Second Shift

_____

_____

Serpent

Snakes of smoke skinny into mouse's nose.
he halts, twitching a nostril to take its measure.
Once, wood-planked water-wheels
powered the mighty turbines
spewing great plumes of steam
soaring to melt into that boundless blue.

Then, black-shouldered shovels
stoked mountains of coal
into blast furnaces
raining ash and soot down
into the lung of the earth.

Oil, gas, the magic spark,
all had their day, turning
heat into light, pulp into page,
flax into frock coats, copper into coils.

Even the tiny atom was indentured
yoked and whipped and branded
till it split apart howling in fury.
Thus man made goods to feed men,
and mouse thrived on their leavings.

Sometimes the smoke went awry
blowing back in men's faces.
There was the stench of meat and charred bones
and more men came in their stead.

Some men breathed fire
sneaking a cigarette on break
flicking the live ash as they hastened
back to their machines

Mouse sniffs all around.
This new trail of gauzy heat –
what lies at the other end?
Will it, charmed, wind lazily upwards
to weave into the gray pall overhead
or snap its tail, rattling
the timbers and bricks down?
Mouse waits in a corner, trembling.

Coffee Break

Jean Jacques looks at the clock
9:52 – close enough.
He grabs a mug
and fills it to the brim
The alarm had socked him
at its usual reveille
No matter how long the day
he has woken at the grey hour
when cats are returning
with pay from their shifts
clenched in their teeth
and salary men are still
glued to their beds.

34 years Jean Jacques
has manned his station
punching in a little before 6:00
to check if the machine
needs lubrication
or a tighter belt
He leaves at 4:00

He is used to this
Only Sundays does his schedule change
Mass doesn't start till 10:00
The Lord is merciful
but Jean Jacques has reported
to Ted Kehoe so much of his life
he's used to serving two masters.

This morning's coffee is thick and sweet
Jean Jacques swallows the last of it
and washes it along with the breakfast dishes
so much to do
Before rousting Elise and Joanna
from bed, he'd fried them eggs
and packed them lunch.
After walking his daughters to St. Joseph High
he'd cashed his last check

and stopped at the laundromat
separating their frills and whites
from his oily uniform.

So much to do
before picking his girls up at 3:00,
like get to the Unemployment Office by 1:00.
He spreads the newspaper across
the kitchen table – the English
is still hard to make out,
especially abbreviations,
but Jean Jacques knows
how to work hard
His drugstore glasses slide down his flat nose
his calloused finger touches
the General Jobs column
and slides down the page –
the tip is already dark.

Scrap

I got no beef with the new guy
just with the folks who brought him on.
Seems tough enough, and hungry –
That's what they look for.
I'm no fool.
Quite a machine – Web IV
hustles lots quicker than me.
I know four of him only needs one college boy,
a computer box, and that fix-it tech who flies
in from Virginia. Easy on the bottom line.

Sorry, each of us old guys needs four hands –
that's a lot of mouths to feed
and each mouth got mouths at home
What's gonna happen to my boy Jimmy?
Steve, Arnold, Julio, Pierre?
Where will they go?
Robert's still got two in school
Wants them to get more learning
than he ever got. Guess the kids will
never know how to stretch a belt
or run a jack. Guess they won't miss much.

Don't fuss about me. Had a good run.
Besides, these old joints need more
than a good lube job can fix,
and the years of paper dust
got me downright mushy.
No use crying over spilled glue.
Still, set me up in the morning,
I do you right – raw paper in one end
Tri-color folders flying out the other
Chunka chunka chunka – there you go.

Sure – I'm a machine, name is Man-Roland.
I don't got feelings, but I got a hunger.
Feed me, I will work for you,
I will give you my life.

Hack Job

The bones of the body
are cracking
one by one
their marrow sacked
in a welter
of downsizing.

Hack,
one machine operator
on the dole,
hack,
two secretaries
shopping with food stamps,
hack hack hack,
three departments
decapitated

How will the body live
with no framework
to hang its flesh on?

The boss just twists
the tourniquet
so we don't bleed dry.
Who will stay the axe?
Who will trim the stumps?
How will we learn
to walk again?

Parking

The lucky ones punched in on Monday
one by one, all on time.
Plenty of parking, Mahmoud said,
his mouth a scimitar,
his eyes, behind safety glasses, dark.

Maria sat in the cafeteria
next to an empty chair.
She'd finally got a shady spot
where her '96 Chevy wouldn't cook.

Jasmine rubbed her calves,
less of a hike now
especially when it's wet.
Fatima would be glad for her,
one of them shouldn't get soaked
in the rainy times.

The foreman is talking to Abner
whose brother is home with the want ads.
We only need happy people here.
How do you see it, my friend --
is the parking lot half empty
or half full?

Third Shift

_____

_____

Good Bones

What a fine old building
ceilings to die for
and that exposed brick
is all the rage.
We can call them
'artist lofts.'

The condos on the river side
will go for what, half a mil?
Wonder what they used to make here –
car parts, blue jeans, envelopes?

Let's salvage the old signage
and mount it in the foyer.
Yes, maybe sink one of those
antique presses
next to the front gate

It will be so quaint.

76 Properzi Way, Somerville

Mr. Flores' carport is roofed in vines,
the oldest older than his firstborn,
thick as a wrist, yielding shade
and hundreds of liters of wine.
He'd hauled the steel pipe ends
from the mill across the tracks
and latticed them over the driveway
of his new-built house.

It was 1964, Portugal already a poor dream
João Flores had Filipa, a job at the mill –
soon babies would fill their new rooms.
Into the rocky soil beside the white-washed walls
he dropped dry seeds, watered, weeded,
and wove them, strand by strand
till a thick mat of purple-scented heaven
hung, August after August,
above his Chevy's and Fords.

Now, retired, he has more time
to tend the vines, trundling
his oxygen tank up and down
the driveway, buttressing the pipes and vines.
It all hangs heavier now,
the doctor says no drinking
so the grapes fall unpressed,
staining the old cars purple.
Mr. Flores pats his vines.
He is still waiting for grandchildren.
He shuts his eyes, and inhales.

Nursery

Mouse still breeds
on the shores of the Merrimack,
still brings her brood good things
from the overgrown brush.
She thanks the Overseer
for sparing the weeds,
red-tinged ivy, spiky thistle
and the flaming sumac.
Few folks tread
and those who do
leave only empties.

In the winters
mouse burrows with her family.
She rations out the hoarded seed
and fills her babes with tales
of monster mouse-holes, dust-mountains
and near-death encounters:
the spray, the traps, the kicking foot,
highways of heating ducts,
and, night and day,
the pounding concerto
of compressors and clanking belts.

The mouse pups huddle together and chitter.
Across the narrows, street cats prowl.

Overtime
_____
_____

Firing Uncle Hillel

If I am only for myself, what am I?
And if not now, when?
                 ~ Hillel the Elder,
                   Ethics of the Fathers, I, 14

Firing Uncle Hillel wasn't as easy as Marvin Fafnir
thought it would be. He'd done his landsman, Reuven
Beatman, my grandfather, this favor long enough.
God is great, God is good, God troubles himself to
help those who trouble themselves not to trouble Him
too much. As Marvin Fafnir tucked away the remains
of his toast he could hear the words roll off his
brother Shmuel's tongue, time and again. Shmuel, or
Sam – he'd altered himself like a suit. Who'd had the
moxie and the vision to get the family out of Ukraine,
then, five dollars in his pocket! – to launch Fafnir
Ball Bearing Company, but who only lived to see the
first lot, like munitions, march off the assembly line.
Marvin owed it to Shmuel to keep the factory afloat
– even if it meant relieving the slow-witted last son of
his best friend from his menial tasks. What if it were
his own son?

Marvin settled his brown fedora down over his brow,
gave Ethel a peck on the cheek, and set off for his 8:15
am shave and trim at John's Barber Shop, down on
Arch and Third. Reuven would be there – he always
was, better than a Swiss clock, John always said.
Reuven and Marvin had gotten their chins nicked by
John almost since they had staggered out of U.S.S.
Lusitania steerage back in '11, blinking at the alien
light after weeks in a dim, teeming rat hole. They
were just smooth-cheeked boys then, Marvin recalled,
stroking his night-roughened jaw as he strode down
Chestnut Street. Boys with eyes pinned on the future.
He chuckled to himself, picturing Reuven arguing,
with what little English he had absorbed aboard ship,

convincing the Ellis Island doctors that both their little sisters' pinkeye was a mark of beauty in Ukrainian girls. Probably just wore those docs down – Reuven had that knack. Funny, how they never spoke of the old days, even though they belonged to the same Piater village landsman, or kinsman, society. The members seemed to have tacitly agreed to function as a community of old, but focus on the new, bringing over what families they could, dispersing small business loans in turn, teaching night classes, and, more and more, burying the old and not-so-old in Beth Alom Cemetery on New Britain's west side. New world, new rituals, why, Marvin didn't even make it to shul every Saturday nowadays – had to make random spot-checks at the factory to keep his foreman on his toes. He trusted Al Cooper, but it was Marvin's name on the sign out front, after all. And on each and every box. What he never missed was his 8:15 shave with John. And Reuven.

Supply prices, competition, all those returning soldiers looking for jobs – Reuven would understand. "I understand, boychik." Reuven clapped his old friend on the shoulder and called him by his boyhood nickname. "Business is business, right? No hard feelings – I mean it." Reuven wiped off the bit of lather that had transferred onto Marvin's suit coat, smearing it further.

"Tell Rachel I'm sorry – Hillel's a good kid – never late, never groused about doing the same job over and over, not like some of these shmoes. It's just, we got new machines coming in, plus-which, it doesn't look right when customers come in – you know what I'm saying…" Marvin stuck two fingers down the neck of his apron, trying to loosen his tie.

"…Hillel's not too quick on the uptake – it's not like I don't know it – been that way since… he was a blue baby, y'know, and we couldn't afford much of a doctor in '27… It's been pretty hard on Rachel, all

these years. She'd hoped to have more, a daughter!
– almost did, but we could barely keep Eddie, Buddy
and Hillel in shoe-leather, as it was."

Marvin did know – he'd said the blessing over the
wine at all the Beatman brises, just as Reuven had
said the benediction at Fafnir's own six naming
ceremonies. L'chaim, l'chaim, shouting 'to life!' and
raising a glass to rejoice the bringing of life into a
Cossack-free world. It was the best a man could do.
Poor Reuven, saddled with a boy who would never
bring nachas, that unique parental joy, or take care of
him in his old age. Ah, well. "See you tomorrow, God
willing." They parted at the corner, Reuven heading
down Third Street to his job at the Sheriff's office, and
Marvin up Arch Street to the factory. As he opened his
ledger, he thought, at least Reuven wouldn't have the
burden of paying a college nut for Hillel. He called his
foreman into his office. "Al – I gotta job for you."

* * *

New Britain, Connecticut was known as "Hardware
City" in those times when a family could rely on
manufacturing to put a Sunday chicken on the table.
Men – Mayflower descendents and immigrants alike
– operated the heavy machines that ran twenty-
four hours a day. From the favored first shift, which
allowed a man some semblance of family life, to the
graveyard shift, which provided a paycheck and a
foot in the door to anyone fleeing his past, the city, in
1947, was a heart that circulated fresh red blood. The
unions were so strong that even the few non-union
jobs paid pretty good. A small house and a used car
were within most folks' reach. Of course, on any
sailing of such a post-war ark, there were bound to
be those who didn't understand each other, as well
as those who had packed along their desperation,
a snarling parcel tied up with string. My Grandpa

Reuven, who had only studied Talmud, was hired on as Constable, collecting rents and making sure the bars closed on time.

Now, as Constable, my Grandpa Reuven had tangled with too many men who lacked hope. He knew if you talked straight and dealt straight with a man, he'd have a running chance. So he'd talked straight with his firstborn, Eddie, hard as it was with the boy always twisting and squirming like a leashed puppy. Eddie had eventually twisted his way loose, right after the war, all the way out to Los Angeles. So much for a boy wearing his papa's shoes. Didn't come back East much, but he married and ran a novelty store, raising a boy of his own. A mensch, in his own way. Buddy – ah, Reuven had been toughest on his middle son, Buddy, my dad. Buddy was the one – bright as a penny and, from day one, bound for college, medical school, whatever it took. Reuven hoped, once Buddy was a doctor, that he wouldn't end up looking down on his unschooled old man. Fact was, even now, Buddy didn't traverse the scant thirty miles home too much anymore. Maybe he'd gotten used to not having the lingering odor of fried cabbage and caraway wallpapering a cramped apartment. At least he didn't insist Reuven call him by his given name, Bernard, like he did everyone else. Would he make his own father call him 'Dr.', when the time came?

Hillel was the son the God of his fathers had sent to test him. When the tiny baby came early, cord wrapped around his neck, gasping for air, Reuven, like Job, cried out why? Wasn't it enough that they didn't have two nickels to rub together? Would their fragile new life in this country, cut so sharply from the old, grow pink and fat, or would it shrivel, gray, strangled? Reuven held his tongue after that, put his faith in God and his own stout arm, kissed his wife and held his newborn son. He named him Hillel, after

51

Rachel's late father, as well as after the ancient Rabbi who said God would forgive any transgression of holy law for the sake of saving a life. Reuven hoped the Rabbi was right, if it came to it.

He never questioned God again, even those terrible times when Rachel had drunk the weed teas to stay barren. You had to hold a baby like Hillel more than ordinary babies – in fact, you could never really put him down. Ever. Where would she find room in her arms for more? She couldn't, wouldn't go through it again, and Reuven didn't know if he could either. They had to think of their three boys' prospects. Grandma Rachel spoke of the two lost souls but once. I only know this from my own mother, who, newly pregnant and worried her firstborn might turn out taking after her husband's brothers more than him, apparently was taken aside by her mother-in-law for some straight talk of her own.

That night, Reuven had to tell Hillel he was losing the only job he might ever hold. He took him into the overstuffed little parlor and sat him down. Hillel knew something wasn't right, as the family rarely sat in the parlor, normally filling up the spare, warm kitchen as they returned home at dusk, one by one, from their day's labor. It wasn't like Papa to sit there without saying anything. In fact, Mama said he cranked open his mouth before switching on his brain, sometimes. The sofa plastic crinkled as Hillel fidgeted, waiting for his papa's words. What had he done? He knew he often didn't get things right, try as he might.

They stayed in the parlor for a long time. Sure, Hillel was sore about the news, and said some words even he knew were bad. What would he do all day, stay home with Mommy like a baby? He liked giving her his paycheck, even though he couldn't make out all the numbers on it. He liked giving his money to the grocery clerk, after his mother had counted it out. He was twenty-one years old.

Next day, for the last time, Rachel packed Hillel a couple of baloney sandwiches and Reuven took him to say goodbye to the guys and pick up his last paycheck.

* * *

Meanwhile, Fafnir's Ball Bearing was unnaturally quiet for a Wednesday morning. Steam wasn't rising from the smokestacks, and the conveyor belts weren't clanking out their steady stream of ball bearings bound for bigger factories in Detroit and St. Paul. Marvin's office was chock-a-block with men.

"Hillel walks, we walk. Hillel works, we work." Max Krajewski folded his arms. "It's like that."

"But he's just a retard. Let him go." Arnie Thompson sputtered. "What do I care? Why'd you keep him on when you wouldn't hire my friend Phil? And now Phil's wife Dot says she'll up and take the kids back home to her folks in Hartford if he doesn't get work."

"Cause Phil's an alkie from way back, couldn't keep a job if his bar tab depended on it." Carl Peterson hit the ball back at Arnie. "Guess I'm sticking with Hillel. He's worked here longer than me. Longer than Joe, here," he said, prodding the man beside him who was finding the floorboards unusually interesting. "Never caused a lick of trouble. Never mouthed off, never stumbled in half-cocked, like Steve, there. And you gave Steve another chance."

"But Steve is the best operator I got. Runs a line like the machine was his lady love."

"Well, Hillel keeps the floor safe, sweeping and hanging things up right." Tony Costello threw his hands up and batted at the air as if it were a foul ball. "And dammit, he's the nicest guy in the world, always joshing like he's your best buddy and handing out sandwiches like they were dimes and he was John D. Rockefeller hisself! Remember, Josey here couldn't speak the English too good at first when he come up from PR, but you didn't throw him out on his can."

The office fell silent. Sid Roth looked like he was nursing a bad tooth. Finally he muttered "Don't look at me, just 'cause I'm a Yid. Way I see it, over here, each man's got to stand on his own two feet." His mouth jammed shut and, tucking his left hand under his right elbow, he went back to clutching his upper lip and chin with the right hand like a vise grip.

Marvin tried to lock eyes with his secretary through the frosted glass door. Marian Tibby hunched over her desk, suddenly too busy to pick up Fafnir's signals as usual. Sure, she'd been afraid of Hillel at first – everyone knew those people couldn't control their urges like normal people. Little by little, as Hillel came daily to empty her ashtray and sweep away her crumpled carbon papers, she'd found that he treated her more decently than most of the guys – his eyes never dropped below her collar and he always called her Miss Tibby. Still, she took care never to be alone with him. You never knew. She'd started thinking, though, about how her father and mother had always seen fit to keep their big Joey at home all the time, before they'd finally sent him away.

Marvin's office was not built to accommodate so many men. They all seemed to be holding their breath. Tentatively, Frank Malone, a short, wiry mechanic, tapped his wristwatch, uncrossed his legs, and got up off the floor. He'd just started the week before, up from Pennsylvania where the mines were closing. He shook his head. "Well, fellas, Fafnir's the boss, he can do what he wants. Let's get back to work."

"Al?" Marvin figured he could count on his foreman to keep the men in line. "You know how labor costs are jumping…"

"Labor costs my keister!" Marvin sat up at the blast of Al's bark. "You couldn't write a check big enough to make up for coming in here every day and not seeing Hillel's funny grin. I work for you, Fafnir, to feed my family. My little brother Henry died of the cough. Hillel's my kid brother now. He's all of our kid brothers. Look, Fafnir, you know ball bearings, right?" Marvin shrugged. "So you know even well turned-out ball bearings are worthless if they don't got a casing of nice thick grease. That's Hillel – he's the gunk makes the rest of us turn good together. Without him, we'd just be a bunch of clowns scraping and grinding against each other. The wheel wouldn't turn. Maybe he don't count so good, but we can always count on him. You're the boss, Boss, but if you've already made up your mind, then when you sit down to do your figuring, figure out how to make ball bearings all by yourself."

* * *

Turns out Uncle Hillel wasn't fired, not by a long shot. Twenty-six more years he punched in at Fafnir's, after first Grandpa Reuven, then Grandma Rachel, passed on, till his pension kicked in and he could live off it like any regular guy. Of course, whenever the count was off on a box packed for Philly or Scranton, the guys would pin it on Hillel, twirling a finger beside their ears, but just kidding-like, like ragging on your kid brother. I know, I do it all the time.

This all happened long before the term "developmentally disabled" had been coined – all I knew was I'd inherited the shame of having a retarded uncle, in a family of otherwise overeducated Jews, the shame a striving off-the-boat family had to bear. Had the evil eye followed us here, despite the finger-spitting and studious withholding of self-esteem building compliments? Great – we had the dumb uncle, whereas my dad had had an uncle who'd been mayor of our small town. Things were not moving in the right direction.

Uncle Hillel, in my memory, always seemed a little too squat and a little too pear-shaped for a man – his eyes sagged down at the outer corners, like he was forever squinting to see something better. And, compared to the rest of the Beatman clan, he grinned way too much, for no cause. Dad sometimes said Hillel had the best life of all of us – no responsibilities – nothing to keep him from sleeping through the night. Nonetheless, if you took a step back, made your eyes as unfocussed as Uncle Hillel's, all you saw was a Beatman.

Like all Beatman men, Hillel was stocky, had a perpetual five o'clock shadow, and a genius for getting his way through humor, bargaining, or just plain bull-headedness. It would have been called chutzpah in someone with more of a gift for words. Hillel was a Beatman, through and through, brain and limbs fueled by the same Ashkenazi blood, sensitized by generations in Diaspora, that had sent his granddad Israel, along with countless landsmen aboard the Lusitania, first to Amsterdam, then London, New York, and on to New Britain. They raced, one step ahead of the Cossacks, wired with the best instincts of any herd, heads up at the encroaching smell of their forest home burning. No looking back – nothing to look back on but the scorched stumps of what had been, to peasants and concert violinists alike, a shared culture, a life. Uncle Hillel was always cadging money from my dad to satisfy his weakness for candy and good shoes, as if following some limbic survival manual.

And now? Hillel just turned eighty, having lived longer than anybody'd dreamed, and he's living the life of Riley up at St. Mary's Home in Hartford, despite his diabetes, charming candy bars off the nursing aides. Got a girlfriend there named Shirley – met on a bus trip down to Florida back in '74 or so. She's slow too, and they've had the grandest love affair I've ever been privileged to witness.

New Britain is crumbling. From a peak of 24,000 manufacturing jobs, 18,000 of which were unionized and the rest at or near union scale, the city now has fewer than 3,000 such jobs. Fafnir Ball Bearing was consumed by the Torrington Company in a hostile takeover in the early eighties. Turns out Torrington bought the plant only to shut it down. Sold it to the city for a buck – thought it was a fair exchange for pulling all those jobs and taxes. There's talk of turning the old Fafnir Co. site into a "Smart Park", hopefully enticing high-tech companies that would offer only a few high-skill jobs to the now-numerous un- and underemployed poor of New Britain. They figure 750 jobs will be created, at best.

We'll see.

Epilogue

Copyright

Like a page on fire,
elbows cocked into question marks,
Leyla Chang invades my dream
strips the white sheet
from my body
plucks the pen from
my twitching fingers
What's this she says
about you writing my life?
since when did I
become a page number
in your table of contents?
Since when did I volunteer
to furnish your castle
                honey
who died and gave you
the right to copy me?

Lisa Beatman, (after her job was outsourced to a community college), is now managing adult literacy programs at the Harriet Tubman House in Boston, MA. She won Honorable Mention for the 2004 Miriam Lindberg International Poetry Peace Prize, and was awarded a Massachusetts Cultural Council Grant, as well as a fellowship to Sacatar Institute in Brazil.

Lisa's work has appeared in Lonely Planet, Lilith Magazine, Hawaii Pacific Review, Rhino, Manzanita, Political Affairs, and Pemmican. Her first book, "Ladies' Night at the Blue Hill Spa", was published by Bear House Publishing.

She may be reached at lisabeatman@yahoo.com.